Ruthless Love

Ruthless Love

DAVID SUTCLIFFE

Library of Congress Control Number:		2019906517
ISBN:	Hardcover	978-1-9845-9010-7
	Softcover	978-1-9845-9009-1
	eBook	978-1-9845-9008-4

Print information available on the last page.

Rev. date: 07/01/2019

To order additional copies of this book, contact:
Xlibris
800-056-3182
www.Xlibrispublishing.co.uk
Orders@Xlibrispublishing.co.uk
797085

In memory of Ruth Elisabeth Sutcliffe
1959—2018

With sincere thanks to Equinox for sponsoring this publication.

Please support Pancreatic Cancer Action and
help find a route to early diagnosis.

FOREVER IN THE GRIEF CAFE

What's a grief cafe?
My five-year-old grandson is curious
about what me and his mum
have been discussing over dinner.

Well, it's a place where we can talk and talk
about the people we love who have died.
Like Grandma?
Like Grandma.

It's been a while now, and maybe
people who didn't know her so well
might get a bit bored
of us always talking about her,

but we don't stop missing her,
and we don't stop loving her,
and at the grief cafe
we can talk and talk about her—

and about how much we love her,
and about how sad we feel,
and about how much we miss her,
and about how much we'll *always* love her,

for as long as we need to.
Oh, he said, speaking the truth
as only children do,
you might be there forever.

WHEN I SAY SHE IS A FIGURE
OF BLESSING . . .

I do not merely mean that we are comforted
by wearing her old boots or
by pressing her fleece to our cheeks . . .

I do not merely mean that she is echoed
in the gestures of her children or
in the kindnesses of her friends . . .

I do not merely mean that we are guided
by imaginary conversations with her
about reading maps or dripping taps . . .

I do not merely mean that she is an icon
to be contemplated in a silent afternoon,
softening our hearts with gentle tears . . .

I also mean that we have a friend
in the high places of heaven and heart,
forever willing us to lose ourselves in joy.

HONEYLOVE

When they told us that honey
could not be sourced for our table
every day of the lengthening years,
we did not believe them.

But maybe they had a small point:
some mornings the jar was empty,
and we drew from yesterday
or borrowed from tomorrow.

But mostly they were wrong, as heather,
honeysuckle, lavender, and wildflower
honeys dripped from our dipper,
forever sweetening life's daily bread.

I wish you all of these and yet more:
Tasmanian leatherwood, orange blossom,
fireweed, buckwheat, manuka, eucalyptus
and sweetnesses beyond our fading world.

So when they softly sigh and sagely say
that sweet honeylove is not for every day,
do not believe them, but neither forget
how faithfully the honeybee labours.

SNAKE

You knew he was there from the start:
from tales, rhymes, myths and legends;
and from the dark moon's steady rise.

You'd glimpse him in the long grass,
coiling insolently from the orchard
as an August evening cooled.

You saw his face last autumn
as he reared at the head of your bed,
his red eyes betraying intent.

Your wide scream allowed him in,
his snout darting to the back of your mouth,
his wiggle smooth and charming.

Breath is forced between scaly body and
soft throat walls. A panic seizes your gut
as you stare at the length of the brute:

a body not your body sprawls
into yours via your lips, snakeskin
scattering sunlight into colours galore.

His tail is metres away, and his full girth
could only be accommodated
by a dislocating of your jaw.

And now that your stomach
has grown familiar with fruitless retching
and the distant world buzzes with life,

it seems he only gets thicker,
longer, as you swallow and swallow
and your hands get to work

at whatever they're supposed to be doing.

REVERSE ANIMATION

I have been looking at those photos I took of you
swimming in Derwentwater on that bright weekend,
which, Google tells me, was nearly three years ago.

In the first you are a long way out, but I know
your dear face from a few fleshy dots set
against the water's granite grey and cloud white.

If I zoom, I can see your glad-to-be-alive smile
blurred and the living white splashes created
by your agile arms, and I too am glad.

Each photo might be a single frame in an animation
of you coming back to me. Now I see your chest
and shoulders, still swimming I suppose;

and now you are wading, tilting forward,
most likely thrown off balance by some
underwater rock; now your left hand

is extended, spraying an arc of water,
your right dipping into the beguiling lake,
your whole body straining forward to me.

Ripples emanate from you in the next,
your thighs clear as you stride,
shaking your hands and glancing down;

and then you're looking at me, a subtle smile
your response to life's goodness, as knees emerge
from the water you loved, a dark wobbly reflection

preceding you. In the last you look off to one side
modestly as I enjoy for a few seconds the curve
of your hips, the slightness of your shoulders,

the loveliness of your dishevelled tresses;
the sinews at the base of your neck;
and the light caressing all the edges

of the body that you always so generously gave.
Now I look at the set in the opposite order.
First you stand as large as life itself

and then gradually grow smaller and dimmer
till only a few pale pixels suggest your likeness and
you are home between the mountain and the lake.

HOLDING HANDS OR MAKING LOVE

not how many days, hours, minutes, and seconds
we spent doing it
but what it represents

we are one

we shook on it habitually

IF YOU WERE WATCHING . . .

you'd see me as a statue in the kitchen,
holding our granddaughter's cup in a tea towel,
frozen in sorrow for minutes at a time.

You'd know that in memory I was running my finger
along your deft, barely there eyebrows
and brushing your downy face with mine

as your smile made your countenance
the shape of love and invited gentle kisses
on each finely shaped fragrant cheek

and a soft, lingering kiss on your modest lips.
Then you'd witness my eerie whines and sobs
as I considered that I will never again embrace

your delicate and sturdy frame in my arms
nor marvel at the perfect width of your hips
nor rest my tired brow at your gentle breasts

nor encircle your excellent ankles in my fingers
nor laugh as you splay your toes like a frog
nor enfold your hand in mine as we walk

nor feel your dear head resting on my shoulder
with your right foot hooked over mine as we welcome
the coming goodness of sleeping together.

PHOTOGRAPHS

I printed more than a hundred,
placed several in frames,
and dotted your image about the house;

now with your loving-the-outdoors look
after a long walk in the hills,
hair joyously dishevelled;

now softly ravishing
with rouged cheek at a wedding,
fascinator on your head;

now handsome on the phone but looking at me,
wearing a smart dress in the sunshine
of an Edinburgh park at festival time.

The one I have placed by my bed
shows you with hair pinned back,
looking to the right with a guileless smile.

What are you doing?
Attending to a child?
Delighting in existence?

In ancient times, tents and temples
were made to pin the gods down;
they didn't want them roaming just anywhere.

My photographs fool me into thinking
that I know where to find you,
you who are everywhere and nowhere.

TELECOMMUNICATIONS

When Javier emails from Buenos Aires
I want to sit in a street cafe he'd know
sharing icy beers in Argentinean sunlight
then resting in the shade of his big old soul
after he has first crushed me like
the great smart bear he is
squeezing the hard nut of petrified grief
into something just a little bit softer.

When Barbara messages from Cayman Brac
about evening beach boules with Robin and Doug
I want to lob silver balls across that bobbly sand
after another hug across time's frontier
with the body that clothes her bright soul,
gently and deliberately and unhurriedly
grasping another of the shifts in our lives,
shifts as indifferent and frightening as the sea.

When Jonathan texts from deepest Hertfordshire,
I want to dance with little Beatrice and Florence,
and without my wife; I can make believe she
is sipping prosecco with her friend on the patio;
then I want curry with him in Tring again
to examine a few of the uncountable desires
that newly widowed clergymen
are not imagined by many to entertain.

When Ann misses her sister and video calls
from Vancouver, I want to walk long, high trails
with that brave counterpart to my late lover
to miss her in solidarity, lost and scared
on a dizzying mountain track,
heads in the blinding whiteness
that lingers somewhere just underneath
the indefinite boundary of the sky.

When Derek calls from cold Helsinki
I want to ride the city trams with
that gangly slo-mo giant of an Englishman
to hunt down missing tigers from the island zoo
after he has shaken my hand
and told me how awful the whole thing is
how utterly dreadful
how absolutely horrible.

TWIN TRAVELATORS

I guess I am on the left-hand one,
studying my unlacing trainers,
my hands now tugging my hair,

now feeling the roughness of the spiky stubble
on the side of my face or scratching bare thighs
or mopping the moisture at the back of my knees.

I'm blinking away over-bright ads and
mopping the moisture at the base of my eyes,
but in my peripheral vision I see

some faintly familiar fellow traveller.
His left hand holds a briefcase, and he stands
in shiny shoes on the other travelator,

a small smile almost on his lips,
his grey suit cheap but businesslike,
his eyes a green–grey–blue like mine,

his hair in a neat cut, his chin jutting ahead,
closely shaved. He's humming a song
by a band I once loved in the seventies,

and for a moment there's a greeting in my throat,
but his track is so much faster than mine,
and he would not hear me. I can just make out

his right hand fishing a passport from his
inside jacket pocket, which sends my own hands
into a flurry, patting pockets to find what I seem

to have lost. He has it—that other fellow—
but he's already scanned it and is successfully
presenting the correct face to the approving camera.

IRIANA

Our three-year-old granddaughter climbs on to my lap,
easy as a dog settling into her basket,
rightful as a queen lounging on her throne.

Her face is shaped like yours, and strands
of her wispy blond hair spiral about
over a thinly covered warm scalp.

She's as wilful as your little sister
and as moody as my old mum,
but her moves are true like yours;

as precise, deliberate, and determined as
a careful actress playing virtuous Perdita;
as you moving always as you.

I drop my lips and kiss that little crown:
the smell of freshly washed wispy hair
twirls around and inside again and again.

FACING UP TO IT

I dodged you all day, but then,
wearied by your frequent overtures,
I relented . . .

I ran a bath, lit a candle,
and the dark heat held me
still at last.

I didn't expect you to climb in,
grasp my face, and stare
eyeball to eyeball.

SCATTERING ABOVE LADYBOWER

Like a child you'd beautify garden plants with fairy lights;
    here for the moment, a snowy powder silvers heather.
You stepped through our lives with a ballerina's grace;
    just now I saw a shapeshifter dancing in the spring air.
On an April peak, I stare at hill and water
    as at a landscape strangely changed. I tried
to shake from the box as high as the heavens,
    yet the day wore a rare calmness, so your airborne ashes
longed to fall to earth like earth was truly home.
    Alone I rejoin the group, a man softly changing,
    leaving you in every place and me confined to one.

KEY IN THE DOOR

Just for a moment
your key is opening the door
and you return home.

This morning I saw you standing
still on the stern of a vanishing ship
looking back at me.

Were you pale or overlit?
I couldn't read the image
in the pearl light of heaven.

I'd supposed we'd meet daily
in the great union of prayer.
Shouldn't you be there by now?

Shouldn't you be here?

BITTERSWEET

A thought experiment:
Imagine a swapping of states.

Me framed by photos and heaven.
You cooking dinner for one.

I'd not want to watch you sad,
a lost and lonely weeping widow.

Call the kids!
Eat with a friend!

Go for a swim!
Such would be my commands.

Now. How you liked me
to sing in the kitchen!

So I dance alone and sing
as my casserole slowly cooks.

It's a new recipe.
The root vegetables you'd expect—

but the flavouring is fresh.
Copious sea salt for tears,

rosemary for remembrance,
dried sage for old wisdom,

sliced apples for love's sweetness,
cider to uncoil the brain,

and a reckless dash
of some exotic bittersweet spice

I found in an unlabelled paper bag
at the back of those drawers of yours.

I don't know what it is
but I've used it rather a lot.

In time I almost grow to like
its complex, pungent shock.

TIRED

I am so very tired, my love.
What grim hard work is grieving!
Fitfully grasping after
things that are bound to be leaving.

I am so very tired, my love.
True rest's beyond conceiving.
Being half a sundered couple
I get half a night's sleeping.

My eyes close at midnight
my mind at half past one
my eyes break before the dawn
the soul work still undone.

SPIEGEL IM SPIEGEL

Last night, my darling, I listened to that CD—
the one you bought me in Guildford.
It's so thin—just piano and naked violin
by an Estonian whose name I can't pronounce,

the piano's slow momentum in time with time itself;
the candour of the violin tones indecently
examining the wrinkling brow up close, mercilessly
scrutinising the creased secrets of the soul.

I am entranced and appalled by the way the tones
are left to resonate together—uncovered, leisurely.
It's not a bland echo of electronic frequencies
but a host of tiny disagreements magnified

a thousand times and yet made purely beautiful
because they are organically true. And so now
I see you again as in a mirror in a mirror,
infinitely far yet grasped in every movement

of my body. And today I know you're here.
As I touch your maroon jacket hanging on my door—
the one I bought you in Leamington Spa—
the rain weeps in a shaft of afternoon sunlight.

RESURRECTION CHILD

Two screwed-up balls of white tissue paper,
one in each pocket of your waterproof jacket,
are found when our daughter tried it on.

Naturally she put them in the bathroom bin,
then we ferreted through your outdoor stuff
to see what she could use for the pilgrim's walk

you'd planned to do with her this summer,
chalking up another of the long-distance hikes
you two have done since the Coast-to-Coast.

The gear was all neatly folded from last year:
your pack-towel for outdoor swimming,
hats and shorts and high-grade walking socks;

and yet that stripy fleece you wore
so often was stuffed inside-out on the top
as if you had only just stripped it off

your warm body after a hike through the hills
West of Catbells or a brisk breezy walk
round War Memorial Park last October.

Scripture tells me you don't need tissues now:
you're a death-defying child of the resurrection,
neither married nor given in marriage.

But the two white balls lie on my shiny desk.
I might need them. I might want them.
I haven't reached that other coast yet.

OLD TIMES

When I imagined you flying over the sea
to be with all the ones who love you in England
I thought of you and her and me
making porridge and loose-leaf tea

and pootling off to a National Trust garden
and walking through herds of truculent cows
happy in the knowledge that she was here
so all of us were safe and free.

And now she's dead, but I got to dream
that when you dropped in for a day or two,
naturally she'd be here again as well,
and you and she would happily be

knocking about the house, peeling vegetables,
slicing fruit, opening tins of tomatoes,
and tugging at strands of truth
as I set the table for three.

So when you said you could not stay with me
for the sake of propriety
(of course I must agree my dear, reluctantly)
this was another little loss for me, you see.

A COVENTRY CURRY

We sat in a booth of the upstairs curry house
with a fizzy rosé from the shop over the road
and three tasty dishes on the table between us.

The fogs of loss have beset our friendly harbour,
but with a courage born of trust, our words
set out into the moving waters of the soul.

You shared your vision of her—
your loving friend, my loyal wife,
who died five infinite months ago—

emerging from a cave in jeans and sweater
to lead us safely home: you, me, my kids . . .
It won't be easy, but it will be OK, she'd said.

And later we entered a silence, like a ship becalmed
in an eerie stillness, and your tear-laden eyes
were alive with a terrible sadness.

How I wanted to reach your hand and speak,
but it's hard to find words that are true to a heart
confused by the sweet sorrow of grief,

and the table clutter kept us apart. So I held
your gaze instead to share for several long seconds
the naked pain I saw there in *your* heart.

It won't be easy, but it will be OK.
You say you three-quarters believe it.
Maybe that's as good as it gets for now.

SHE'S NOT HERE . . .

Imagine an old stallion
still in a stable at dawn
the door wedged wide open.

Imagine a pretty songbird
singing dirges in a cage
open to the heavens.

Imagine the perplexed women
making a vacant tomb
into a kitsch Jesus grotto.

Imagine a solitary widower
stooping with photos and flowers
while outside a fresh wind blows.

DEPOSITION

Helsinki Cathedral

Jesus's body splits the altarpiece,
gently cradled by the men,
bystanders watching,
women waiting.

His pose is close to something
that could be captioned
'woman reclining on bed',
but his skin is coldly grey.

So the two golden angels
look demurely away,
unable to contemplate
all that beauty bore.

Last time you and I saw this
I guess we stood
side-by-side, hand-in-hand,
and softly talked.

Today my moist human eyes
will not leave the holy corpse
being tenderly received
by Nicodemus and Joseph

ready for burial.

DREAM AFTER SIX MONTHS

After our two eldest grandchildren
had eaten potatoes and beans
and nectarines at our table,
and played tig in the heat of our small garden,
and washed with some of your quality soap,
I settled them to sleep on the old mattress
we bought thirty-six years ago in Leeds,
on which their mother and uncles were conceived,
and countless stocking presents were unwrapped
by children fumbling at the magical edge of the real.

I pulled the sheets around their little bodies
as you would have done
before coming to our newer, bigger bed
and falling into a dreaming doze,
dreaming of a knocking at the door.

I opened to find you
—how my soul sang—
though you stood cold in your long grey coat
with your bright-blue scarf round your neck
(it was winter when you left us);
cold and confused,
distressed at being out so very late,
and away from us for so very long.

BELLY

Listless from being fed cake earlier
by women who have already lived
two or three decades longer than you
I burst from our house and ran free.

A little jog? Instead I cut a wide arc
through the south and west of the city
skipping past the mansions of Earlsdon
round to my favoured urban park

which I take clockwise for a change.
I feel the hardness of my sternum
the hardness of my ribs
the hardness of my shoulders

the hardness of my collarbone
and the hardness of skull and brain
as I sprint by two lovers
then jog past Larkin's school.

I dash sun-blinded into a bright field
and on to streets of terraced
houses guarded by ranks of tightly
packed parked cars and vans.

Tempted to languish a little I recall
the voice of our second son
urging me faster as I near the end
so on I fly into the setting sun

blurring watery eyes making it tough
to cross the humming roads as cars
keep blocking my path like guillotines,
and a hint of a death wish sweetly

floats through the prelude to night
like a translucent petal of a rose passing
away on a zephyr, and then I'm home,
lying on the floor, belly rising and falling,

soft as kindness, warm as sunshine,
bare, tender, rounded, human, loafish, old,
laughter's cauldron, stubborn store
of tender fat for wanting yet to come.

PREPARING TO RESUME PREACHING

I am wearing a nicely ironed shirt
under a thick woollen cardigan—
it's been a cold, cold winter, my dear.

So the shirt is largely hidden, but
believe me, its crisp frontage does
enrobe my chest very neatly.

I learnt to use the steam setting
at the weekend, vapourising
the awkward creases

under the arms and those opposite
the opening where
the sleeve splits to allow a hand

to enter a cuff before fastening.
How diligently I attended
to the minor undulations

half-hidden under buttons
and how carefully I flattened
the collar that all can see.

I'm practising for standing
at a pulpit. How you frowned
at shoddy work in church

and liked to see me
nicely presented in
smooth, clean cotton shirts.

RIGHT-HAND GIRL

My own right hand has been bereaved;
its only love has ceased to be.
It has no tear ducts, tongue, or brain;
it reaches out and squeezes air.

GRIEF LIKE A DROP OF GREEN INK

A large drop of something like viscous green ink
splashing into a glass of milk,
a moving stain coursing through the fluid
drawing the eye to only itself:
a dark intrusion on what had been
simple and childlike and wholesome;
a complication; a disturbance;
a gyrating, disintegrating, disruption
of a previously settled state . . .

Stir, stir, and the once pristine milk
may, in time, absorb the lurid impurity
until it becomes a sophisticated tint
barely noticeable to a new observer,
supplying a hint of an extraneous mystery
when the whole is tasted,
a complex additional flavour,
hard to place, gentle, subtle,
neither pleasant nor unpleasant,
perhaps redolent of the odour of
muddy dead leaves trodden underfoot
after a night of heavy November rain.

ALLIUM

Raindrops shine on the allium's generous bloom
which is, at first glance, an ivory-white globe
with a soft tint of green set on a sturdy stem.

But look closer. The surface of the sphere is
comprised of dozens of linen-white six-pointed stars
made of mini petals emanating from green centres

each with several tiny yellow pollen-bearing
stamens perched millimetres out on white filaments.
Dozens more neatly folded miniscule buds are

poised to open at some secret sign from soil or air.
My heart is glad you buried this bulb last year,
a slow-burning invitation to sense and desire.

A blackbird sings. The tips of the lavender
you planted for your old dad are colouring
towards purple. The honeysuckle I bought

you is set to burst into beauty on arching twines
rising well above my head. The allium may reign
for a little while yet, but thunder already rumbles

across the city and white light excites the air.
Heavy raindrops begin to form. Orange
California poppy petals are the first to fall.

LOST IN SPACES

On a two-day break to comfort me,
I feel your presence awaits me at home,
decanted into your dressing gown,
your toothbrush,
the shiny silver shoes you recently bought from Rieker,
our kettle,
the half-used box of lemon and ginger teabags you liked,
our unmade bed,
your half-charged laptop,
the shopping list you'd lately written,
the bulbs pushing up in the garden,
the lavender you planted for your dad,
the bright Caribbean bag you used for chargers,
the vases you kept,
the great quantity of frying pans you needed,
the hand-me-down wardrobes we have tolerated too long . . .

You are in the softness of the abandoned clothes encased within,
in the space between the front door and the kitchen
in the refreshing space of the shower
in the sunlit space above the vacant sofa's seat
the space between the gate and the door
in all the empty spaces between walls and walls.

I must get home.
You'll be missing me.

LAST WORDS

You emerged from the morphine fog
and inhabited your eyes again
for just a few moments.

I love you so very much, my darling
I said, or something very like that,
something unoriginal and true.

You took a long breath and gathered strength
and spoke once more to me, your husband
of thirty-five years.

OK.
No more
could be said.

HIGH SNUG

In Heddwch house, Arthog, Wales

I sit in the window seat of the high snug.
Below, the waters of the estuary are turning.
Though gentle waves approach the house
and upstream currents can still be discerned,
the general flow now seems to be
away from the land and out to the sea.

The whitish whisper of wind and wave
is sometimes breached by a seabird's cry.
Silent hills smudge into grey clouds
but flatline down by the wide river's shore.
Sunlit sandbanks are seen again now
and foamy waves break on beaches reborn.

And I conjure you sharing my comfortable bench,
your back leaning on the opposite wall,
our feet resting by each other's thighs,
touched now and then by affectionate hands.
I love to imagine your body still here, though
this physical dream is near too much to bear.

Tonight the waters will rise up again,
and the river will gape as wide as a sea,
and I know you'd be swimming in its cold embrace
or be doing some task we'd left undone.
You'd not be still with me, softly sensing how
the same old tide returns and returns and returns.

YOUR CLOTHES . . .

are hanging around in wardrobes,
a few waiting about on door handles
or lounging idle in a washing basket.

How unlike you they are—the action
woman who had to be persuaded
to sit at the end of a long day.

Smart dresses for family weddings,
fancy frocks for nights out at work,
breathable base layers for misty hills,

the lacy secrets of the lingerie drawer,
socks in a range of fabrics and colours,
everyday pants and warm thermal vests,

intricate fascinators, improbable hats,
sombre black trousers and jeggings and jeans,
smart power suits and frivolous dresses,

prettiest scarves of blue and gold silk,
delicate cardigans in fine woven thread,
bright T-shirts and elegant ivory blouses,

new woollen jumpers and old woollen coats,
faux-leather jackets and glittery trainers,
strong winter boots and sensible shoes:

all lie lazy and listless, lifeless and limp.
Yet these congregations of clothes routinely
manifested the once-in-the-universe you.

Normally I'd meet most of your body
in guises you'd carefully assembled
before your morning shower.

I'd see not your legs but the sheen
of tights under a pretty skirt
or denim shaped by calf or thigh.

But what of that bedtime suit of nothingness,
that warm soul-skin you sometimes wore
to free my imprisoned sighs and cries?

That contoured touchscreen of delight
is now dispersed silver powder
on a Derbyshire hill.

What then of artificial outfits?
Yet I do not fetch the black bags
you kept under the kitchen sink

for the final packing of
your lingering, lifeless,
and lovely old clothes.

COVERED

The door is locked for the night.
I'm brushing my teeth.
But who's that person I feel
standing right behind me?

A ripple of fear as I turn to look.
Nothing to see of course.
It can only be you—you who
always had my back covered.

TEARS AT RALPHIE AND POPPY'S

With our son's wife and our grandson
in a stay-and-play cafe
I wonder what cake you'd have chosen.

Chocolate brownie is my guess,
with a decaf latte. I imagine your eyes
swelling with life to engage the baby.

Then Becky says you really did
come here with them and sat
at that table three yards away.

I almost begin to imagine you,
maybe in your turquoise sweater
and some tight blue jeans.

This beginning preludes a springing
of fresh tears flowing down my cheek
for ten minutes in the corner

of the cheery child-friendly cafe.
You *were* here. I *am* here.
Where are we now?

Where are we now?
Bowie's question bounces
forever in my skull.

MY HEART IS

A fraying nest
An empty chest
An inaudible scream
A hazy, listless dream
A weaver of lies and denial
A busy creator of cant and guile
A restless seeker in an endless game
A silent actor forever mouthing her name
A wanderer trapped in half-remembered years
A subterranean volcano of isolated hot tears
A drunk offering his old shirt for the moon
A house of tissue in a raging monsoon
A refugee from love songs to forget
A mulling mix of guilt and regret
A tiny yacht in an ocean swell
A steel marble in a bagatelle
A light-years-distant star
A sealed and empty jar
A severed live cable
A Christ-less stable
A bleeding stump
A howling chump
A falling cat
A fool
A fool
A fool
A bloody old fool

3:35AM, 1ˢᵀ FEBRUARY 2018

Your body still,
breathless at last.
Something gone.

This was better than
the afternoon and the evening
and the half night of strange breathing

sounding sometimes like drowned messages
called by a girl from a departing train
(It's just the vocal cords vibrating,

said the nurse), and sometimes
like the raspy whimpering of some
small woodland creature in a cruel trap

(It's just some fluid not draining right).
I lay in a bed by yours, holding your hand,
wondering whether to sleep or wait,

not knowing if this was the night
we had been waiting for or just another
disjointed night of dozing and waking

in which I must aim to muster the energy
you needed from me in the morning.
I wished I'd known for sure

that death was dawning and there'd be
no morning again for you, my darling.
Then I could have been more precise

about the timing of your final breath
and been sure to hold you tight
as you glided out of that night.

But you'd died to this world at the
raise of the morphine hours before.
Perhaps your spirit hovered in our prayers

that last evening. I'm pretty sure
you didn't hear who the killer was
in the thriller I finished reading.

In fact I think you'd just about gone
a day before when the terminal
agitation gripped you and you sent me

on fools' errands—anything to stay living—
mark this card, bring me a cotton bud,
get the nurse to sit me up a bit,

get the nurse to sit me lower in the bed.
Dave, you called me, for the first time
ever in thirty-seven years

and talked of your dad
not to think of heaven
but to reassure yourself

you'd done right by him
when he had been dying
a couple of years before.

Fetch me more water; brush my teeth.
Before one task was done
you commanded another

—it's in Ruth's best interests
to raise the dose—
I was in no position to argue.

And now the dreaded moment has come.
Would I shout in loud rage
at some impotent divinity?

Ruth, there was a kind of beauty
about you then. It lasted
for twenty minutes, I'd say.

It was so much better
to see this illusion of Ruth
silent and still, no longer

animated by pain, no longer
debilitated by cancer
into a woman for whom

walking to the bathroom
with a frame and a nurse
was a triumph—

you who took
mountain ranges
in your stride—

now just dead.
This was better than
you being so very sick.

To hold you—
what of you was in the bed—
for some precious minutes

almost as if you were clinically dead
but spiritually still lingering,
strangely beautiful.

But as time passes, I think
the whole thing was so much worse
than anything.

EVERYONE LEFT WITH YOU

It's not just you that I miss—
yet it can only be you,
you & your two dead parents,
& mine, & my dead brother.
It could never have been you
because you are the only constant
in my equation.
It's not you, but it can only be you.
Your loss is all loss.
Losing you is losing everyone:
our eight dead grandparents
& sixteen greats before them
& thirty-two before them
and forever back to faces that might be yours
living centuries ago—yours and mine—
to that moment of shared begetters
inevitably lost long ago.
To lose you is to lose them all.
To lose you is to lose myself.
Everyone left with you.

ULTRASOUND

Music plays in
an easy succession of
our sort of songs.
I want to break free . . .
The doors open.
Her ultrasound scan is done
but she waves me away.
That room is only for patients
she later explains.
So I stand and watch her from the corridor.
She's walking down the aisle in her wedding dress.
She's giving birth to our children.
She's waiting for the GP to ring our doorbell.
Wake me up before you go go.
Her skin is yellowing.
I have seen an angel.
Her manner is tetchy.
Every breath you take I'll be watching you.
An invisible barrier has descended
across the entry
between ultrasound waiting
and ultrasound scanning.
What more in the name of love?

WELLS

This one has slaked my thirst
for thirty-five years
with its easy winding action
and its water fresh and sweet.
But now its private supply
has suddenly dried.

Dozens of you told me
no worries come drink
at each of our wells
with a sip here
and a sip there
your mouth will stay moist.

Then there's the forgotten spring
most have buried with busy living
bubbling unheard
flowing unseen.
I have sipped there many years
but now its water is rock-hard.

HOW TO SCREAM WITHOUT DISTURBING OTHERS

Go into the bathroom.
Bolt the door.
Lean over the sink.
Disengage your vocal cords.

Test with an unvoiced whimper.
Tilt your head back.
Open your mouth very wide.
Trust to sheer breath.

Project a stream of negative energy
from your volcanic heart
through your dry throat
into the bathroom's private air

for several long seconds.
It should sound no louder
than a heavy sigh.
Let the sink catch any drool.

Try not to look in the mirror.
Wash your face
and dry with a towel.
Repeat as required.

HOW I MET YOUR MOTHER

4 October 1980

Our first day out involved
a steam train, a Yorkshire moor
and a burnt-out car.

We played in the happy wreck
then called like Brontë's wayward ghost
on Oxenhope's overlooked moor.

She was delighted and appalled
when I scrawled speech bubbles
on the Ordnance Survey map:

Heathcliff! Cathy!
It was almost sacrilegious
and very unlike her decent dad.

Kate Bush was our soundtrack
Southern Comfort was our drink and
Safeway was the supermarket

we popped into somewhere near
Leeds central station. I was stunned by
the speed of the tasty spag bol

she created at Clarendon Road
and then words arced like limitless confetti
till almost dawn and we were children

at holiday's start. *What do we do now?*
she wanted to know. This was it.
How do we manage to stay alive

with such a deep flood of delight
drowning the stuff of the day?
Not getting it and being heavy-eyed

I merely said 'Sleep.'
Thirty-eight years later
the holiday has ended.

We'd said we were either
in love or insane. Looking back
it was mostly both, I think.

URBAN LOVERS

Sunshine all day!
So let us walk about the city
as we always liked to do.

Distant buildings would draw your eye,
teasing you to disentangle connections
in matted urban geography.

We'd thread through narrow paths
between six-foot garden fences
opening onto a dusty pub

by a rugby stadium or into a little park
by a canal. It's how we found
our penultimate house, remember,

just wandering through Bristol
as we've wandered through Leeds,
Venice, London, Helsinki, Paris,

Florence, Edinburgh, Assisi,
and latterly Coventry.
No place quite like home.

It's early April in Coventry now,
and my right hand has again forgotten
to remember that you're gone.

I will trust it as it reaches.
Which way now, honey?
Tugs and squeezes will lead me

as if searching for a certain place.
In the new Jerusalem we always
wander winding lanes lit by

the light of only love
because there is no place to go
from there.

DAVID, DEREK, AND MINUS RUTH

I sit at an airport bar,
waiting to fly to Finland.
Last time, you came too.
Tonight I sit alone.

The x representing you
is still in life's equation
but is now known to
have a negative value.

David plus minus Ruth
eat noodles in a bar.
I can do negative numbers.
They have their own rules.

So long as you don't
become a zero, I can cope.
Me plus zero equals? Me.
Me times zero equals? Zero.

Time to board the plane.
You coming or what? Again
you leave me to pay though
you used to do all that stuff.

Queuing to step on board
your absence sticks close,
just behind me on the right.
Put your boarding card

and your passport in the
zip pocket of your bag.
In Helsinki we will
take in a concert,

attend an English play,
sample the film festival,
eat cake by the sea—
me, Derek, and minus Ruth.

MEALS PLAN, FOUND BY THE TOASTER, ANNOTATED

Mon Scone pizza
Your familiar printed hand in pencil organises our food for the week ahead.

Tue Panzanella Salad (Dad & I are out to eat)
That was your last proper meal out with friends.

Wed. Risotto.
The list uses the margin of some old work spreadsheet.

Thur. Lentil + veg soup + bread
Your punctuation is inconsistent.

Fri . Lasagne
The GP came round to discuss your blood test results.

Sat . Stir fry
We spent the morning at the hospital, but they wouldn't admit you.

Sun. Sausage, mash, Yorkshire puds.
You never wrote such a list again.

Mon
You managed a bowl of peas for tea.

Tues (12th Dec)
You vomited old blood, like coffee grounds.
You spent a night on a trolley in A and E.

Weds (13th Dec)
You were told you had a tumour on your pancreas that had pushed into your duodenum.

Thur (1st February)
You died in the early hours (seven weeks later).

RUTHLESS LOVE

You died,
but the love I bear you did not.
Not only does it carry on,
but each day it is ever more strong.

Yet if a surgeon with a skilled hand
offered to excise you from my brain
like a cancer,
I'd turn her down.

I did not wish to live
without your presence.
Now I cannot wish to live
without your absence.

Mine is a pitiless love
that will not let me go.

FALSE FIRE

Leviticus 10:1–2

Nadab and Abihu took their censers,
put fire in them, added incense, and
offered unauthorised fire before the Lord.

My wife's body was destroyed by fire
authorised by her own living lips,
and then fire died away, died away . . .

. . . so I have taken my golden censers and
kindled the false fires of daydreams,
quick fixes, and imaginary love talk,

and they have kept me living for a while,
brightening lonely midnights
with a cheery artificial glow.

Fire came out from the presence of God
and consumed Aaron's sons,
along with their little fires.

I did not know that the
consuming fire of God could be
so dark, so cold, so merciless.

MEETING WITH COLLEAGUES

Thick glass walls contain the pressure.
Inside, my head throbs, but I can see them,
and they look very like real people.

They behave as if they can hear my words,
and politely ignore the gulping, bubbling
noises that must attenuate my speech.

Their words are heavily muffled
by the gallons of water in my head tank,
but I can often make out their meaning.

No one says they're pleased I'm back
or they're sorry for my loss. After all
it happened nearly four months ago,

so we get on with organising stuff.

THE HALF-BIRTHDAY PARTY

My eyes open wide to you in the darkening air,
and alluring as a blood moon, you linger
in the crowd of unobservant partygoers.

Their eyes are on the host, who is
addressing his guests about cake,
his eyes like theirs, too narrowed to see

your stunning dress, your bold lipstick,
your winsome smile of approval and pride
gracing his life with a lost sister's blessing.

On his birthday six months ago, wheelchair-held,
you'd looked as tentative as a ghost,
your dressing gown and showy sunglasses

lending you the air of a faded star as,
over a supermarket cake, you'd wished
him happy birthday one last time.

But now, in the twilight of the half-birthday,
our mouths laughing amongst the trees' shadows,
your countenance presents a bright benediction

for those with eyes to carry on seeing,
and those with ears to carry on hearing,
and those with hearts to carry on loving.

IN THE SUMMERTIME

Fatuous minutes slip by my flesh;
my phone says eight have passed away.
I can feel them like steam singeing my skin.
Let it burn, says my brain, let it burn all day.
Now nine more have skimmed away.

The temperature's rising; the air is thick;
a computer says an hour's passed by;
I have no clock, I hear no tick;
my sweat smells sweet, my gut is sick.
It's work to breathe when the air's so thick.

All over the world the hotness is brooding;
earth on the stove with death in the pot;
death by flame, death by smoke,
death by exhaustion, and death by denying
the planet is sick, and it's too damn hot.

But how can I care for the Greek seasiders
fleeing to the beach from wildfires in trees,
dying by the dozen in neat family groups—
when she, my sun, my impulse and dream,
my reason, my lover, my friend and my queen

is gone? Flimsy seconds like sparks from a fire
flit all around me and die in the air.
Listless months devoid of desire
are crafting a man unlikely to care;
a preacher framed as a rag-and-bone liar.

DREAD

That awful knot in the stomach's core;
    that queer liquidity at my centre of gravity;
that intuitive fear I am quarry to be caught;
    that sharp nausea at the dank smell of dawn . . .
is either the desire for self-extinction
    rearing its all-too-reasonable head
or an impudent shove to leap for life
    beyond the advent of my lover's death.

Or is it both? Must something more be killed
    in me before the path of life may lead me on?
Am I clinging to a form of you that's gone;
    absurdly cherishing an empty urn,
    like a Mary Magdalene holding tight
    to a beauty rising from earthly sight?

SURRENDER

I feel as if my hands are on my head
and I'm kneeling on a cold concrete floor
watching intermittent tears landing.

My ingenuity is exhausted; I see now
there is no escaping my singular self.
I am an 'I' and not a 'we'.

A body can survive without a breath
for two, three, maybe four minutes—
but not for six months. Fool!

My wife's body was incinerated,
her ashes blown abroad by the four winds
and dispersed into thin air.

I sometimes comfort myself
with notions of heavenly reunion,
but she will never walk the earth again.

I'm alone. I've lost. It's over.
No substitute rises from the bench.
I surrender myself to myself.

GREY AND ORANGE

As I peep through the curtains
greyness is raining on our street.
I lay out some of my new clothes—
grey underwear, grey shirt,
grey socks, grey jeans,
and an old knitted grey sweater—
and head for the shower to rinse off
the lingering darkness of night.

Dry and clean, I drape
the inert greyness
all over my skin,
but then add,
against the cold and for the eye,
the burnt-orange fleece
you bought me two years ago
in the new year sale.

PHANTOM DAWNS

A solo traveller sniffs the air,
noting a hint of a turn in climate,
a marginal rise in temperature
felt on the skin of his lined face.

The shaft of sunlight breaching cloud
was only a bashful, wishful flight
of some hopeful quarter of his mind,
but still his eyes now scan for light.

He descends the steep drop from
the mist-beset hanging valley,
quickly picking, sliding, and falling
his risky path down moving scree.

In the murky twilight, the next mountain
rears before him—impassable,
sodden, massive; white cataracts
gaily festoon its numerous crevices.

Whose voice projects the lonely cry?
A bird of prey circling and circling,
a singled man searching and searching,
a dying woman greeting fate?

BY THE RIBBLE IN MAY

A vast snowdrift of new-flowering wild garlic
flows down the beech-wooded hill
blurring into an impression of
pure white joie de vivre.

Bluebells shimmer in sycamore woods
and late primroses splash colour
on to the banks of the bronze river
as it oozes forever to the Irish sea.

Up in old Settle, the walk began
and there the Royal Oak still stands
where we first shared a bed
nearly thirty-six years before.

And on and on, my legs must walk
where your eager feet no longer tread;
and hard and long my eyes must gaze
at wonders lost to the sight of the dead.

GRIEF BIRDS

Wings a shock of yellow,
body dun and big;
one bird on my patio
with a tear for each eye.

Its mate flies in, a fatter thing;
and then another;
and then some more, each one fatter
than the one before.

It's tough to see
with stinging eyes—
but feel the fluid, flying mass
of a crushing murmuration.

And then dusky silence;
the empty air;
a lately set sun;
a cold breeze.

ANNIVERSARY

Only the men came down to breakfast at first,
two with children eager to play,
the rest of us blinking and yawning
our way through tea and toast.
The women slept on like you,
who slept and rose without me.

A couple of days ago, women and men
larked in the sea off Barmouth,
losing ourselves in salty waves filled with energy
and watching a mist approach from the South
and the sun just occasionally
refracting through the frosted tops of breakers.

A strange anniversary! How to mark a marriage
that might be seen as dead, when I yet live.
We painted a pebble for each of our years
to hide on lofty Welsh crags and in urban gardens.
My first attempt blurred into shapeless yellow
That must have been about 2008.

WYMING BROOK

The energetic peaty brook
explodes over great grey stones
then dashes into sunlit pools and
squeezes through slender runs,

foaming and roaring unstoppable,
unstable, yet following a path known
since anyone can remember
through the mixed woodland

of pines and birches, hollies and oaks.
The fallen trees add to its sport,
presenting playful obstacles and making
fresh frames to view the sunny water

through, until they rot where they lie
or are swept downstream
past pink flowers of herb Robert,
and blue flowers of forget-me-not.

BROUGHTON LAKE

The regal copse of high trees sweeping
in a pleasing arc at the lake's far side
is darkly mirrored in the square of water.

It's a giant glass, sometimes etched
by raindrops sporadically scattering
on to its otherwise impassive face.

At a far corner, a half-dozen swans
emerge into the open expanse,
dipping heads into a secret world

of earth particles suspended in water,
before receding into a narrower strait
apparently propelled by sheer willpower.

The trunk of a lime tree supports my back,
a mass of its heart-shaped leaves an uneven
wobbling frame for my skewed corner view.

Though hundreds of its leaves lie dead
at my feet, very many more thickly block
the sky above, reducing it to fragments

of white heaven glimpsed between the
green leaves of earth's old trees
till winter shall clarify the vision.

Patches of vegetation float in islands
at the lake's centre and form a sludgy
beach-like fringe to one of its shores.

A year ago your arms held a toddler,
keeping her shaded from hot sunlight
at the other side of this tree

as we laughed at the antics
of two jaunty festival jugglers.
Today I look the other way.

I stare at the reflected shapes of trees
and at the negative sky-spaces
reflected in white around them.

The afternoon rain was heavy and long.
Now it comes and goes by the whim
of the blank bank of featureless clouds.

DREAM AFTER EIGHT MONTHS

Someone had a video clip of you—
a fragment from an old Nativity play—
would I like to see it?

You were walking with children at church,
wearing a cloak of bright stars on inky fabric,
a wise woman with a golden gift.

Your face was tired and weathered,
but your expression contented gentleness
as you moved at a little child's pace.

What a lost treasure I'd found,
but before you reached the stage,
a voice loudly screamed at me 'Dad!'

I awoke like a diver thrust up to air
after a deep and wondrous
underwater reverie.

I want to be asleep with the dead,
not awake with the living,
but the living keep raising me up.

MANTELPIECE

At the end of a shut-up, tucked-in day
of rolling loss round my body like
a tart wine in a dry mouth,
I stand by the fire and meet you
through an iconic photograph.

No time for a cursory goodnight
I face your smile at the flickering flames
and the particular calmness of your gaze
locks my eyes then irresistibly transmits
serenity or peace or grace or something

in that territory. You look at me deeply
unimpressed and undisturbed by all
the lunacies I had painfully rehearsed today
when thinning out the files of three decades
of marriage and jobs and houses and kids.

You always wanted goodness for me
when you lived in your small body
and now my spirit has imbibed the truth
that your limitless love is a mantle of peace
always resting light upon my shoulders.

FINISHED

He stands still awhile, a long while,
a good, long while,
his brushes drying on the stained table,
one arm folded, the other hand's index finger
looped over his chin.

The nuance of his smile
is blended from a palette of
a fitting pride,
the dusky sweetness of rest,
and a slowly savoured tenderness.

His innocent, wise eyes wander over your image
from the delicate toes
to the grey-and-honey cloud of hair,
and to there, where your heart
looks to be almost beating on.

Maybe one day I'll look at you too
in a fashion akin to this. Maybe
the longing for what is not will stop.
But surely that can only be on the day
when the artist rests his gaze on me,

and I too am perfectly imperfect,
completely unfinished at last,
drying on the canvas,
ready to be mounted next to you
in the gallery of forever.

CHRISTMAS LIGHTS

The true light that gives light to everyone was coming into the world.
—John 1:9

Shiny-eyed, I'll sing the carols she loved,
hearing her girlish, off-pitch voice
bright with wonder at Christ on earth.

Decorations? Just candles and fairy lights
all about our little house. She loved them,
so will she roam awhile on Christmas Eve,

lost and found amongst the sparkling things?
A tree? Perhaps. Stockings? Well, think
how a child's delight lit up her woman's face!

She was one who always glimpsed—
undimmed across unfriendly space—
the Magi's distant star of hope,

a light no darkness ever overcame.
She bet her life that light was true
so let us learn from her and do the same.

TWENTY NINETEEN

The rim of the champagne glass
is a perfect circle bounding
a wee enchanted sea or

a tiny sparkling universe,
perturbed a touch as my right
hand faintly twitches.

Big Ben chimes softly on the iPad
and fireworks dart brightly
within a seven-inch screen.

We enter a year without her. Twenty.
Nineteen. The countdown begins.
We warmly embrace an empty space.

We'll take a cup of kindness dear
for the sake of auld lang syne, and
the cow jumped over the moon.

Lightning Source UK Ltd.
Milton Keynes UK
UKHW010309180719
346343UK00001B/26/P